# GOOGLE ADS IN PLAIN ENGLISH

*Advertising on Google Search, Google Display Network & YouTube*

*For Students, SME's, Start-up, Freelancers & Non-Profits*

2021 Edition

*By: Hassan Imtiazi*

Copyright © 2021 *AIDA Digital Ltd.UK*

All rights reserved.

> "It's hard to find things that won't sell online."

JEFF BEZOS, FOUNDER & CEO
OF AMAZON

# Contents

INTRODUCTION ........................................................................................................... 2

ACKNOWLEDGEMENTS .............................................................................................. 5

FOREWORD BY MIKE BERRY ..................................................................................... 8

COPYRIGHTS & DISCLAIMER .................................................................................... 12

WHO IS THIS BOOK FOR? ......................................................................................... 15

DIGITAL MARKETING ADVANCEMENT ...................................................................... 18

CONCEPT OF SALES FUNNEL – AIDA MODEL ........................................................ 22

WHY GOOGLE? .......................................................................................................... 27

GOOGLE SEARCH MARKETING EVOLUTION ........................................................... 32

THE SEARCH NETWORK ........................................................................................... 38

GOOGLE DISPLAY NETWORK ................................................................................... 74

YOUTUBE VIDEO NETWORK ................................................................................... 107

GOOGLE ANALYTICS ............................................................................................... 126

CAMPAIGN OPTIMISATION ...................................................................................... 142

FREE & PAID TOOLS ................................................................................................ 147

GLOSSARY ................................................................................................................ 150

ABOUT THE AUTHOR ............................................................................................... 152

# 01

# INTRODUCTION

# INTRODUCTION

Hello and welcome to the Google Ads in plain English book. My name is Hassan Imtiazi, and I have been working in digital marketing for the last decade. I have managed multi-million dollar campaigns and generated more than $70 million in revenue for my clients. In 2015, Google published a case study on my work on the *think with Google* portal. Over the years, I've worked with Google teams, various tech giants and digital agencies, and this book is a summary of my experiences.

I have been a Google-certified professional for many years across search, display, video and analytics platforms. In this book, I am going to teach you the do's & don'ts of Google Ads as it is very easy to start campaigns without any knowledge and waste your hard-earned money. I will share a simple explanation of each platform, context as to how they work, the process to follow to build campaigns and then how to optimize. I hope you will find this book beneficial and useful for your future life.

*Hassan Imtiazi*

*https://www.linkedin.com/in/hasimti*

Hassan Imtiazi

# 02

## ACKNOWLEDGEMENTS

# ACKNOWLEDGEMENTS

I would like to dedicate my book to my late father, Ghufran A. Imtiazi, who passed away from liver cancer in June 2019. I have learned a lot from him as to how to be disciplined in life, have excellence in my work and be an honest and good human being.

I'd like to thank my mentors Mike Berry, Rob Thurner and Naeem Raza for always being my inspiration and guidance. And last but not least, my better half, Amaizia Imtiazi, for her continuous support for the last 18 years in my personal and professional life.

# 03

# FOREWARD

# FOREWORD BY MIKE BERRY

## This is a very valuable book.

Paid search: known as PPC or 'Pay-Per-Click' is a unique form of advertising. The searcher has revealed their intent – they are interested in something right now – perhaps they want to buy! The challenge is to grab their attention, standing out on a crowded search results page, to motivate a click and then a conversion – often in a highly competitive market and all at an affordable and sustainable cost per click (CPC).

The author knows this world well. And, as with most things in digital marketing, it is changing. Rapidly. Google launched in 1998, a David challenging the Goliath of Yahoo!. Many things have changed since then, including Google's inexorable rise to dominate search in most countries of the world. In China that accolade currently goes to Baidu. During this period of time, search has gone mobile. Voice and image search are now real things and the future is likely to feature Virtual Assistants powered by AI, along with other technologies and devices not yet invented. These will all impact paid search; search marketers must continue to adapt to the changing search market which is likely to be far removed from the '10 blue links of the late 20$^{th}$ century.

The modern PPC Manager faces many difficult decisions every day – which keywords to bid on, ad and landing page creative, and not least how much to pay per click. There are tools to help, but they need to be set up and managed. If not tightly controlled, PPC campaigns can rapidly consume any available budgets without sufficient returns! Beyond the traditional PPC text ad, Google Ads now offers display opportunities via the Google Display Network (GDN) and YouTube (including pre-roll and mid-roll video ad formats).

Despite the multiple challenges presented by this complexity, marketers know that we all search online to find things, including products and services we want to buy and successful search managers recognize the power of a well-structured and carefully optimized PPC campaign. It is absolutely possible for three players (search engine, marketer and user) all to be winners.

This book is an indispensable primer on Google Ads – how to do it and where it is going next. I recommend it to anyone who needs to know more about this powerful marketing platform.

*Mike Berry*
*CEO & Founder, Mike Berry Associates, UK*
**https://www.linkedin.com/in/mikeberrylinkedin**

# 04

## COPYRIGHTS & DISCLAIMER

# COPYRIGHTS & DISCLAIMER

Copyrights reserved by AIDA Digital Ltd.UK. No reproduction or citation without the consent of the author. This is a completely unofficial book on digital advertising, digital marketing, internet advertising and Google Ads. No one at Google, Facebook, Instagram, YouTube, LinkedIn, Bing, Pinterest or Snapchat has endorsed officially nor has anyone working for these companies been involved in writing this book.

This book is based on my personal and professional experience of working in the field of Google Ads. Any reference to Google, Facebook, Instagram, YouTube, LinkedIn, Bing, Pinterest or Snapchat or any other social media platform should not be constructed as my endorsement of those products, services or tools nor as a warranty as to their effectiveness or compliance with search engines or any social media platforms.

Hassan Imtiazi

# WHO IS THIS BOOK FOR?

Digital marketing skills are in high demand, and companies are actively looking for trained staff to run their online marketing departments. It is now even more necessary for small business owners to understand how online marketing works. With this in mind, I have written this book for anyone who wants to learn Google Ads, be it a student, freelancer, a small business or a non-profit. If you have an online shop, local restaurant or great cause, why not show it to the world and increase your reach and achieve your business goals. This book will also help someone who has recently started a career in digital marketing.

There are two unique things about this book. It is structured in a way to explain each Google platform with context for beginners and how to build campaigns with a step-by-step guide. Secondly, I have shared my personal experience of running various campaigns for my clients across the US, UK and Middle East.

Google Ads in Plain English

# 06

# DIGITAL MARKETING ADVANCEMENT

# DIGITAL MARKETING ADVANCEMENT

**In Chapter 6, you will learn:**

- *How digital has changed our lives*
- *The importance of digital for businesses*

Let's take a step back before I even start explaining to you what Google Ads are and why you should be using them as an advertiser. We don't realize our dependency on technology—imagine you don't have internet for one day: what will you do, how do you carry on your business or how do you even communicate or entertain yourself? I have seen the time from when we used to use a fax machine and dial-up internet services.

Technology has changed so fast that even 10 years back, it was difficult to imagine a phone with a full computer's memory, touch system and HD content. The emergence of social media platforms (Facebook), price comparison websites (aggregators) and on-demand services like Netflix (OTT) is now a part of our day-to-day lives. This has changed how we do business; having a website is no longer just an option, it is a must to have. At the same time, having your business presence on Google is a must whether through a paid medium or through search engine optimization. If customers can't find you on Google, that means you pretty much do not exist.

Even having a website and being on the Google search engine on page 2 is no good. You need to be on top to win the business. You need to talk to your customers, listen to them through social media platforms and tell your story via YouTube videos. This all looks fine, but for individuals, small businesses and start-ups, this is a daunting task as they need to concentrate on so many things but don't have the time to learn digital marketing skills, social media marketing, content creation or shooting product videos.

When you look at numbers, like how many people spend hours on social media, how many watched videos on YouTube and how many are searching on Google for different products or services every minute, you will be amazed. There are so many opportunities that can be grabbed with little effort. This is where my book will help you to understand Google Ads and give you a full understanding when starting your first few campaigns. You know your brand better than anyone, so even if you hire an agency or freelancer, you'll need to be fully aware of what is happening with your Google Ads campaigns. Once you acquire basic knowledge, you will then guide them not only from a business point of view but from audience selection and campaigns optimization as well.

# 07

# CONCEPT OF SALES FUNNEL

# CONCEPT OF SALES FUNNEL – AIDA MODEL

**In Chapter 7 you will learn:**

- *Concept of AIDA Model – Sales funnel*
- *What is an online value proposition?*

Although my book is mainly focused on Google Ads, I think it's a good idea to go through some marketing fundamentals as not all of you who are reading this book have a marketing background. At the end of the day, the goal of any business whether online or offline is to bring more and more customers and to get sales. So, let's understand a few concepts as that will be useful to understand the bigger picture and where Google Ads fit into your business. There is a concept of funnel marketing whereby you as a business define the stages of the customer's journey. One of the most commonly used and classic models which marketers use every day is the AIDA model.

What does AIDA stand for?

**Awareness:** creating brand awareness or association with your product or service.

**Interest:** generating interest so that users can do further research about your product or services.

**Desire:** creating a desire for your product or service through an 'emotional connection'. Move the consumer from 'liking it' to 'wanting it'.

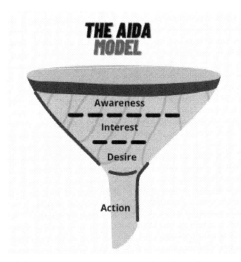

**Action: Call to action**. Move the buyer to interact with your company and take the next step, i.e., buying or booking.

## Online value proposition- OVP

There is no point in advertising or marketing if you do not create some kind of value for your customers. Online is a complex world where customers have plenty of choices, so why would they visit your site and buy from you? Having perfectly structured Google Ads campaigns might not bring the best results unless you have some kind of USP to offer your clients. In a technical way, it is called online value proposition. It is closely tied up with brand positioning within an online context where you as a brand or service provider try to answer questions like *who we are, what we offer, to whom we offer* and *what makes us different.*

So, it is creating a differentiation strategy that clearly states the benefits and sets you apart from the competition.

In recent times, the best example is the Uber service. The app has changed the way we order a cab, i.e., calling cab services where you will find an uninterested operator, explaining where your location, then how much it will cost and how you pay. Uber, with the use of Google Maps, solves this issue, and in just one click, we can order a cab. Now the driver has your pinned location, and you know his name, ratings and payment is cashless. So, your **online value proposition** (OVP), user experience on-site and engaging content—everything counts when it comes to customer conversion.

Now you have some understanding of a marketing funnel and online value proposition, let's dive deeper into our main topic, Google Ads.

# WHY GOOGLE?

**In Chapter 8, you will learn:**

- *Why Google is important for marketers*
- *Google Network - Search, Display, Video & Gmail*

Firstly, reading this book is itself evidence of the importance of Google and Google Ads—that's why you bought this book. In simple words, anything or everything we do on a day-to-day basis is based on certain intent, whether it's ordering pizza, finding a local plumber or finding what is next week's weather or latest news; we just Google it. Every day, millions of people search for answers to their questions, and Google is helping them to get information.

With these millions of queries generated every day, Google is offering services where it is making it possible to meet buyers and sellers. This is done through a self-serve ad platform called Google Ads. Users search for cheap flights to Spain and advertisers start showing offers in the form of Google Ads. More relevant ads and offerings outperform others. On one hand, users get the answer to their question, and on the other hand, the advertiser gets the potential client. Lastly, Google made money based on the cost per click model. CPC is a method where Google only charge advertisers if the user clicks on the ad. So, all three parties are happy in the equation.

Secondly, Google owns the world's largest email, Gmail, and the world's second-largest video search engine, YouTube. This means if someone is listening to Justin Bieber's music, it can be reached out to sell music concert tickets. Recently, people have been watching more content on YouTube through their Smart TVs rather than on normal TVs or live shows.

Thirdly, Google owns websites, blogs and portals and offers enormous opportunities for brands to reach out to as wide an audience as they want and as niche an audience as they like. This network is called Google Display Network or GDN. The funnel point of Google also allows brands to re-market users as their buying journey is complex and based on many factors. This remarketing tool is fantastic as it will allow advertisers to show offers and entice users to convert. You must have noticed some ads chasing you from retailers where you have visited recently—that is remarketing.

Lastly, Google Play is one of the world's biggest marketplaces for app downloads. Cheap data packages and smartphones usage have enabled mobile application marketing boosts recently. Google Maps, Google Shopping and Google Local Business are also key platforms people are using on a day-to-day basis.

Just to give you context, Google Ads is not a relatively new platform. There are two decades of hard work by Googlers to develop and improve it. So, let's go and see Google's timeline.

# 09

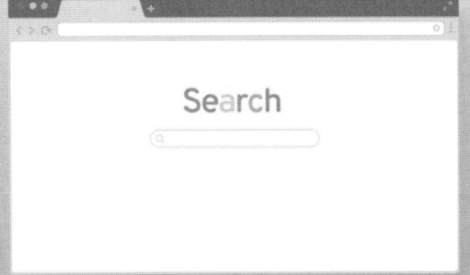

# GOOGLE SEARCH MARKETING EVOLUTION

# GOOGLE SEARCH MARKETING EVOLUTION

**In Chapter 9 you will learn:**

- *20-years' timeline of Google innovation*
- *Products added to Google Ads platform*

1. The evolution of Google Ads goes back 20 years. Introduced in October 2000, Google AdWords at that time was one of the first self-serving ad platforms for advertisers. Initially, the Google Inventory was used to sell on a cost per mile basis where advertisers used to pay for ads to show 1000 times on the website.

2. After two years in 2002, the model then changed to CPC, which is a cost per click. Advertisers then only have to pay once a user clicks on the ad, so it's kind of an action led paying model.

3. Since the Google display network is comprised of millions of websites where brands and advertisers have the opportunity to show their products and services, Google in 2003 launched the Google Ad Sense program.

4. In 2005, site targeting was introduced where ads can be shown to specific sites instead of using only keywords.

5. To show more transparency and efficiency, in the same year, Google introduced a Quality Score as an important metric to rank ads, and this was coupled with minimum bids.

6. In November 2005, Google introduced a free analytics platform (Google Analytics) to track the performance of campaigns. The tool is still commonly used, and its basic version is free.

7. By 2006, advertisers started investing media spend through this platform, and to ease the scale of work and smooth operations, Google AdWords Editor was introduced. The editor allows advertisers to work offline and can do bulk operations at the same time.

8. Demographic targeting was also introduced in the USA in 2006 as well as Google Local Businesses and Maps.

9. In April 2007, Google acquired Double Click, which allows cost, efficiency and scale for larger organisations.

10. In 2008, demographic bidding was introduced.

11. Interest-based advertising started in 2009, where ads can be served based on users' interests, such as shopping or holidays.

12. In order to enhance a Google search and give more real estate to performance advertisers, Ad-Site Links was launched in 2009. Ad Site Links gave the opportunities to show different products and services where users can be directed to unique landing pages.

13. A big leap in terms of pursuing users to convert was made in 2010 when cookie-based remarketing was enabled. This has changed the dynamics of many industries, especially retailers, where they can chase warm shoppers by showing relevant ads and customized offerings. We will go through the remarketing topic in detail in a separate chapter.

14. In 2011, new targeting options were released based on a user's physical location.

15. Combined with Google Crawler technology, dynamic ads were introduced in 2011.

16. 2013, enhanced campaigns were introduced where users can be reached based on multiple factors like location, bid, time of the day and device. This has made improvements in Google AdWords' performance.

17. In 2015, offline customer data could be uploaded in AdWords to target prospects online.

18. In 2016, Google pushed for a mobile-first approach and eliminated right-hand-side ads. That same year, the text ad limit increased from 30 characters to 80 characters.

19. Smart campaigns were introduced in 2017 using Google Machine Learning to give better performance. The same year, a similar audience introduced to-scale campaigns for look-alike audiences.

20. In July 2018, Google AdWords become Google Ads. This new brand represented the full range of Google campaigns including search, display and video.

21. In 2019, Google made retirement of average ad positions. The same year, new audience options introduced affinity and in-market segments.

# 10

# THE SEARCH NETWORK

# THE SEARCH NETWORK

**In Chapter 10 you will learn:**

- *Organic vs paid search ads*
- *Search vs internet browsing*
- *What is a search network?*
- *How Google auction works*
- *Ad rank & Quality score*
- *Keywords & matching types*
- *Search Campaign creation*

## Difference between Ads and organic search results

Let's say British Airways promote summer sales with Google Ads. When someone conducts a Google search for terms related cheap tickets to Budapest, British Airways Ad can appear on the top or bottom of the Google search results pages.

Ad's placement is primarily based on how relevant and useful it is to what the person searched for, bid, quality score and few other factors.

At the same time the other section of the page shows "organic" search results. These are natural search engine results appearing on Google. These are unpaid Ad links and can take users directly to British Airways or other airline website without any charges.

## There is a difference in search & browsing

It is important to understand that there is a fundamental difference between searching on Google and browsing on the internet. From a digital marketing and online behaviour point of view, users browse on the internet across different websites to read content or watch videos, but their intention is not to buy something. Whereas searching for something actively on Google based on the pure intent to buy or doing some product or services research is search marketing. Marketing on search network using cost per click ads are search marketing and placing banners across websites is display network advertising.

Google search network is actually a group of search-related websites or apps where you can place your PPC ad (pay per click). So, when you advertise on Google, your ads are shown on search results. These search results are based on search queries by users. And these search queries are a combination of keywords or phrases which users type into the Google search bar.

Just to give you context, imagine you want to book a holiday in Budapest, what will be the first thing you do? Obviously, you will Google it, and this is where everything started. As soon as you type keywords like 'cheap holidays' into Budapest, Google in a fraction of seconds pulls thousands of search results. Out of these, the first top 4 are Google Ads. Although, there is a perception that the highest bidder always wins, but in reality, there are certain technicalities involved.

From a commercial point of view, it is good for Google to give the place to the highest bidder, but Google wants to maintain a certain level of relevancy at the same time, and that is why it will show results that are close to the user's search query. There is no point if you type in holidays in Budapest and results come up for holidays in the USA as there is no relevancy, and it is less likely you will even click on that ad.

## Google Ads Basics – *Learn the ropes*

In simple words, the way Google works is based on real-time auction where different advertisers bid through keywords to get certain ad positions on Google search results. They bid against each other in a Google auction and pay if someone clicks on their ad. But one question which my clients often ask me is if a click does not mean a sale, which in reality is the case. Google only charges for clicks, not for sales, but business owners want to see more and more sales revenue. This is where you need to learn and be an expert on Google Ads so that you can generate traffic and convert it into sales.

## Search results

Each Google product or platform has its own buying model. For example:

1. **Search Ads (PPC) are sold based on cost per click (CPC)**
2. **Display ads (GDN) are sold on cost per thousands (CPM)**
3. **Video ads (YouTube) are sold on cost per view (CPV)**

## Google Products

There is no doubt that Google Ads is a simple and powerful tool for SME's, freelancers or non-profits to be on the top of Google search results. Based on business objectives, you can achieve first, second or third positions within a few hours depending on the bid, keywords and quality score.

Google Ad Network on GDN and YouTube gives humongous opportunities to advertisers to reach their potential customers at scale. You can market your app or show video ads on YouTube. There is no limit to creativity and audience reach.

Audi display banners on the Guardian website

Gillette display banners on website

## Bidding on Google – *How Auction works*

There are 3 main factors in an ad auction that determine which ads appear and in what order:

- **Bid** - When you set your bid, you're telling Google Ads the maximum amount you're willing to pay for a click on your ad. How much you actually end up paying is dependent upon competition and other factors.

- **The quality of your ads** – Relevancy is the main factor in Google Ads. Google Ads looks at how relevant and useful your ad and the website it links to are to the user against a search query. The main element is the quality score which I have explained separately. The better your quality score means you will pay less as Google will reward you.

- **Ad Extensions -** If you have all relevant ads extension, then Google Ads estimates how extensions and other ad formats you use will impact your ad's performance. So, even if your competition has higher bids than yours, you can still win a higher position at a lower price by using highly relevant keywords, ads and extensions.

## Example of Auction

As per Google Chief Economist, Hal Varian, in one of his famous YouTube videos.

For every successful auction on Google, we need 3 parties.

1. **User**
2. **Advertiser**
3. **Google**

Advertisers want to show relevant ads so that users click on them. User clicks on ads to get relevant information and don't want to see spam ads, and Google wants to make a good experience for both advertiser and user.

For example, I will explain to you how it technically works. Imagine there are 3 slots on Google, and we have 4 bidders in the auction.

| Bidder | Max Bid | X Quality Score | = Ad rank | Ad Position |
|---|---|---|---|---|
| B1 | £4 | X 1 | = 4 | Ad will not show Due to low quality score |
| B2 | £3 | X 3 | = 9 | 2 |
| B3 | £2 | X 6 | = 12 | 1 |
| B4 | £1 | X 8 | = 8 | 3 |

So, what happens every time a query is made on Google, the backend system will run an auction in a fraction of seconds. An auction is run only for clicks as if the user clicks on the ad, then the advertiser will have to pay. The highest bidder will get first position, the second-highest bidder will get second position, and so on.

Looking at the table, you can see all advertisers have set their max bid, which is the maximum amount they are willing to pay. Then each advertiser has a quality score; by applying this formula, you will get an ad rank.

Ad rank = CPC bid x quality score

With bidder no.1 who has 1 quality score but is willing to pay a max of £4, his ad will not show due to a bad quality score. Whereas bidder no.3 who has set a £1 bid only, his ads come to position 3 due to a high-quality score of 8.

**Watch video.**

Watch the video by Google Chief Economist on the Google auction system.

shorturl.at/giD16

## Quality Score – *Tricky Bit*

A quality score is an estimate of the quality of your ads, keywords, and landing pages. Higher quality ads can lead to lower prices and better ad positions. Unfortunately, Google does not tell you the exact guidelines as to how you can achieve a good quality score, but these are few factors.

The quality score is reported on a 1-10 scale.

Main components - expected click-through rate, ad relevance, and landing page experience. The more relevant your ads and landing pages are to the user, the more likely it is that you'll see higher quality scores.

Quality score is an aggregated estimate of your overall performance in ad auctions.

Ad Rank - *Important metric*

It is also important to learn about ad rank here.

Ad rank is calculated using your bid amount and your auction-time ad quality (including expected click-through rate, ad relevance, and landing page experience).

In its simplest form, ad rank is:

$$\text{Ad Rank} = \text{CPC BID} \times \text{QUALITY SCORE}$$

## Keywords - *the bedrock of your campaigns*

A Google search is solely based on user intent, and that is how it works. User's intent and moments that matter for buyers are important elements of the consumer buying cycle. Keywords are *words and phrases* that users search and match with ads. The keyword match types are the pre-requisite whereby Google Ads show your ads in an auction.

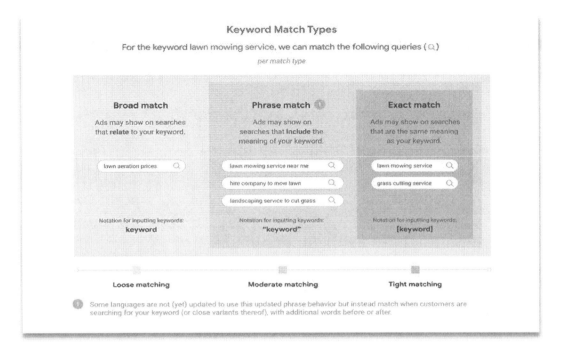

## Broad Match

Broad match is the default match type that all your keywords are assigned as if you don't specify another match type (exact match, phrase match, or a negative match type). I recommend not starting any campaign with broad match as this will eat at your budget. Broad match lets a keyword trigger your ad to show whenever someone searches for that phrase, similar phrases, singular or plural forms, misspellings, synonyms, related searches and other relevant variations. For example, when you add "holidays" as a broad match keyword, you tell Google Ads to try to show your ad for searches containing that term or a similar one (in any order).

Your ad might show for searches on "holiday," "cheap holidays" and "vacations." This is a very broad level strategy and not suitable for everyone.

Example of low carb diet plan keyword. Google will show ad on all search queries related this keyword.

| Broad match keyword: | Ads may show on searches for: |
|---|---|
| low-carb diet plan | carb-free foods |
|  | low-carb diets |
|  | low calorie recipes |
|  | Mediterranean diet books |
|  | low-carbohydrate dietary program |

**Phrase Match**

If you enter your keyword in quotation marks, as in "tennis shoes," your ad would be eligible to appear when a user searches the phrase "tennis shoes," **in this order**, and possibly with other terms **before or after the phrase**. for example, your ad could appear for the query "red tennis shoes" but not for "shoes," for "tennis," "tennis shoe" or "tennis sneakers." this keyword matching strategy is more targeted than broad match but more flexible than exact match.

So, working off of the above "tennis shoes" example, creating a phrase match for "tennis shoes" would result in the following potential matches:

Search queries your ad shows against:

- tennis shoes
- best tennis shoes
- tennis shoes for sale

Search queries your ad won't show against: *Word Order Is Not Same*

- shoes tennis
- tennis shoe
- tennis sneakers

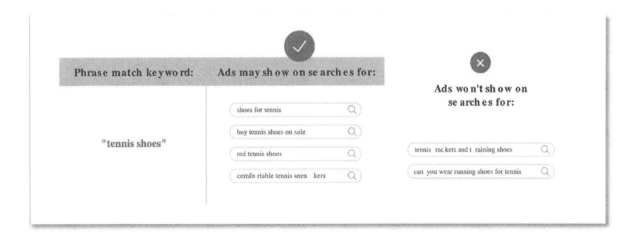

**Exact Match**

After phrase, exact match perhaps is the one of the mostly commonly used matching strategies. Primary reason being it is a more targeted approach, and your ad will be shown to the most relevant search queries. With exact match, you can show your ad to customers who are searching for your exact keywords or close variants of your exact keyword in your campaigns.

The flip side is that keywords you have selected might not have enough of a search volume (exact match), so you will end up with fewer impressions served and hardly any clicks. Generally, CTR for these campaigns is good because of tightly themed keywords.

Exact match is designated with brackets, such as [red shoe]. Below is an example of how exact match will work.

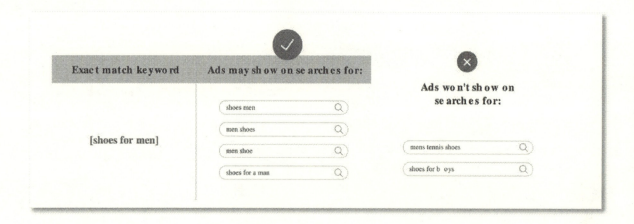

**Broad Match Modifier - BMM**

In February 2021, Google made changes to broad modifier, which I will explain to you in a bit. But in simple words, Broad Match Modifier by its course of action shows ads if the keywords are present in the search query in the exact or close variant form. These keywords are highlighted with a + sign to demarcate that the keyword needs to be a part of the search query.

So, with new changes made in BMM:

New updates on phrase match simplifies match types by combining the control of phrase match and the expanded reach of broad match modifier. The new matching behavior will be more expansive than phrase match but slightly more restrictive than BMM.

For example, the phrase match keyword "moving services London to Luton" will continue to cover searches like "affordable moving services London to Luton." It will also cover searches that traditionally only matched under BMM, such as "London corporate moving services to Luton." For the updated phrase match, word order continues to affect matching behaviour, and ads won't show for searches where the wording changes the meaning of the match (for example, people looking to move from "Manchester to Luton").

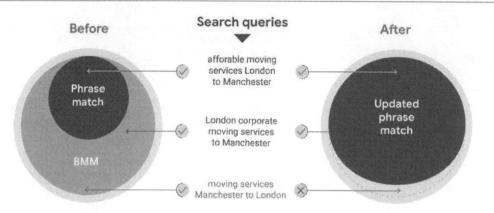

## Negative Match

The goal of every business is to generate sales and get a positive return on ad spend. Hence, cost efficiency is an important metric in your ad campaigns. You don't want to spend on keywords which are not related to your trade or products; you don't want to spend on those keywords which are costing too much and not producing results at all. In this situation, negative keyword match types let you exclude all search terms from your campaigns which you don't want to bid on at all. You can set negative phrases and exact match types in your campaigns but be careful and double check before doing that as this will have an impact on the campaign delivery.

For example: if you are selling long haul expensive holiday packages or business class flights, you might want to consider having the word "cheap" as a negative match as you don't want people who are looking for budget holidays to visit your site.

## Quick Summary for Keywords Matching Types

### Google Ads Keyword Match Types

| MATCH TYPE | SYMBOL | EXAMPLE KEYWORD | APPEARS FOR | EXAMPLE SEARCH |
|---|---|---|---|---|
| Broad match | No symbol | tennis shoes | keyword or large variations + close variants* | socks for running |
| Modified broad match | +keyword | +tennis +shoes | keyword or small variations + close variants* | tennis trainers |
| Phrase match | "keyword" | "tennis shoes" | keyword phrase with words before or after + close variants* | nike tennis shoes |
| Exact match | [keyword] | [tennis shoes] | keyword + close variants* | tennis shoes |

## *Keyword Intent – The Secret to Attracting the Right Traffic*

Keyword intent is one of the most crucial aspects of paid search advertising. *Intent marketing is any kind of marketing that aims to meet an end user or prospect's intent – that is, what they really want or need in that moment of time.* This is what Google calls "*moments that matter.*"

I have seen well budgeted search ads campaigns fail due to a lack of understanding of the intent behind visitors' searches, However, by leveraging keyword intent for intent-driven marketing, advertisers not only attract more customers through traffic on-site but also drive more sales.

## *The Difference Between High Intent and Low Intent Keywords*

High intent keywords are also said to have high COMMERCIAL intent. These keywords show a strong intent on the part of the users and potential of sale, whether it be to buy something, inquire about a service, or another type of action that has a strong possibility of leading to a later sale.

There are three basic types of search queries:

1. Transactional intent searches – searches performed to buy something—most valuable.
2. Informational intent searches – searches performed to answer questions or learn something.
3. Navigational intent searches – searches performed to locate a specific website.

## Research process - So how do you find keywords?

For any given search campaign, you need to start researching about what kind of keywords you want to include in the campaign. High intent keywords with "buy now," "cheap flights" or "fixed mortgage rates" all have commercial significance.

Google's Keywords Planner can pull all historic data for keywords with a minimum or maximum bid, search volume for the last 12 months, region split and device split. This crucial information will help you determine which keywords you want to bid on and with what keyword matching strategy.

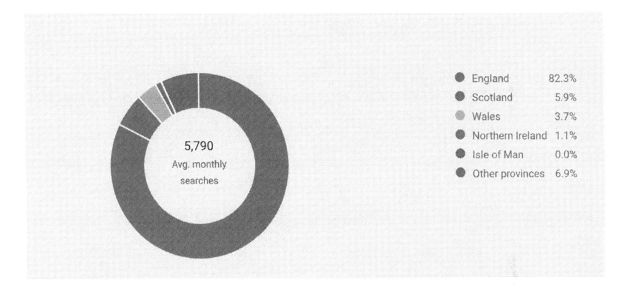

So, you now have a fair idea of the majority of the searches done in England at a certain time of the year (summer holidays). There is low to medium competition with the top bid range from £0.39 to £0.53. You have monthly estimates which will allow you to do a basic forecast about budget allocations for each month.

# Google Ads Campaign Structure: *Laying the right Foundation*

**Google Account Structure**

- **Account**

This is where you will have all of your important information like log in email, passwords, billing settings and account access to others. You need to be careful to whom you are giving access and what level of access. For example, agencies can only have standard access not admin access, whereas an employee can get view only access.

- **Campaigns**

Campaigns are like containers where you have ads, bids, keywords, targeting and other settings. Campaigns are usually categorized based on what you are selling, for example, Apple might have separate campaigns for each products like computers, laptops, mobile phones and accessories.

- **Ad Groups**

Each of your campaigns is made up of one or more ad groups which must be theme based. Ad groups can contain one or multiple ads which share the same targeting. For example, the "holidays to Budapest" ad group should have all keywords related to Hungary or Budapest deals, and ad text should reflect the main keywords. Bids are also set at ad group level.

## *Step-by-Step Guide*

Campaigns Structure is the most important part of Google Ads campaigns so making it right from the outset is really important. It is like building your house on a flat piece of land or renovating an existing house. Foundations, architect designs, practicality of floor plan, interior designs (aesthetic and visual look); everything makes a real difference. Google Ads Campaigns Structure works exactly the same way.

You need to lay down solid foundations to make sure you not only achieve your business goals but at a minimum cost or without losing money.

**Selecting the right campaign settings**

Your goals (traffic vs conversions), budgets (daily or lifetime), campaign type (search or display), location (local vs regional), bid strategy (manual vs automatic), audience selection and frequency capping will all have an impact on campaign performance.

Let's go quickly through how to build a traffic campaign on a search a network. If your objective is to bring traffic, then select website traffic as your goal.

Then select campaign type, for example: Search

The next step is to select the Google Network. For example, search ads can be displayed both on Google Search results (See Pic 2 British Airways) as well as on display sites as a text ad. Ideally, with limited budget campaigns, I recommend to opt-in only search network. If you've selected both, then I have observed that the Google system will spend more on the display network instead of search as the impressions or demand on display is much higher than users searching on Google Search itself.

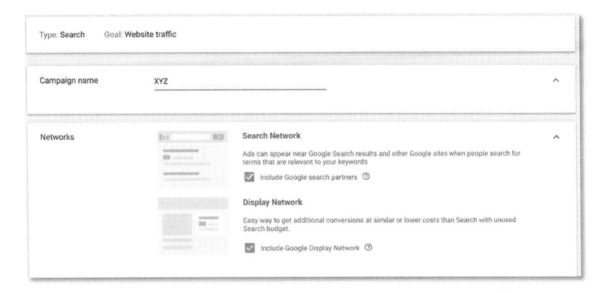

The next step is to select your campaign location. Location settings are a bit tricky because of two reasons.

Firstly, it will give you control of where you want to show ads, so you need to know how narrow or broad you want to go. For example: the local Pizza Hut will only want to target people in Central London postcodes but because of a tight radius, targeting their ads might not deliver (too narrow geo targeting).

Secondly, default settings by Google do not always produce 100% results, and it is a bit vague. For example: the default option will serve ads to a broader audience if they are not in targeted location.

**Reach people in, regularly in, or who've shown interest in your targeted locations (Presence or Interest).**

For beginners, this is not the ideal setting to choose. This option lets you show your ads to people who are likely to be located in, or are regularly located in, the locations that you've targeted.

**Reach people in or regularly in your targeted locations.**

This will then lead you to the language selection. Generally speaking in search ads cases, it is English. Audience selection is not applicable as search ads as we will use keywords only. Set a daily budget of whatever you think is affordable to your business. But it has to be based on keywords you selected and historical CPC which can be accessed through the Google Keywords Planner.

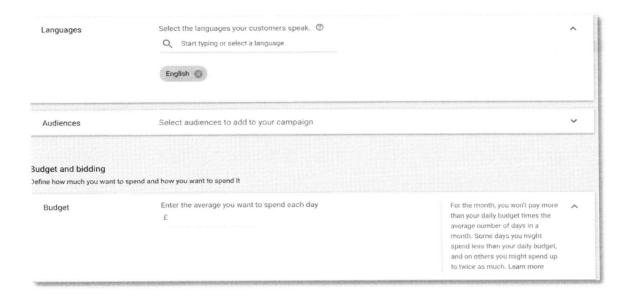

Bidding is an important part of your campaign setting as this will define your competitiveness. There are various options available; for now, select clicks only.

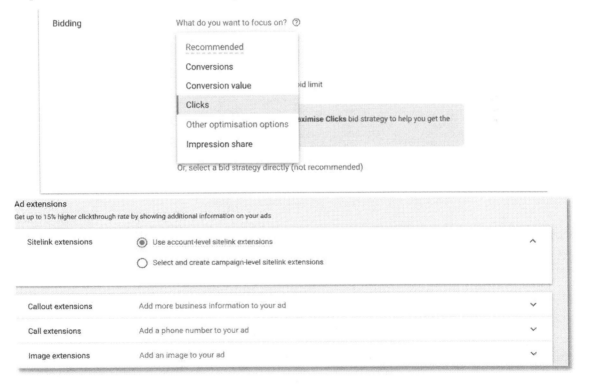

Google Ads is all about getting more real estate on Google Search pages so having more and more ad site links is very strategic. Try to have as many site links, call out extensions, call extensions or images (relevant to your business) as you can. We have seen more than 10% improvement in click through rates having ad extensions.

**Sitelink extensions**

To add more text and links to your ad, there is great way to do that. Google Ad sitelinks allow you to create up to 6 ad sitelinks with unique landing pages. This will give you more opportunities to show offers and products as well as get more real estate on the first page in comparison to your competition.

**Call out extensions**

Similar to ad sitelinks, call out extensions can give more options like promoting your business's USP's. For example, free shipping or 24-hour service.

**Call extensions**

As more and more people access websites through mobile devices, call extension is handy to give out your business's phone number. With just one call, the user can call you directly, hence your click through rate would be great. This will lead to more customer engagement and more chances to convert users into sales.

**Image extensions**

This has now been rolled out in almost all countries. Image extension allows you to show rich and engaging media. These images will show alongside Google Search Ads and Google will pick up the image from your landing page.

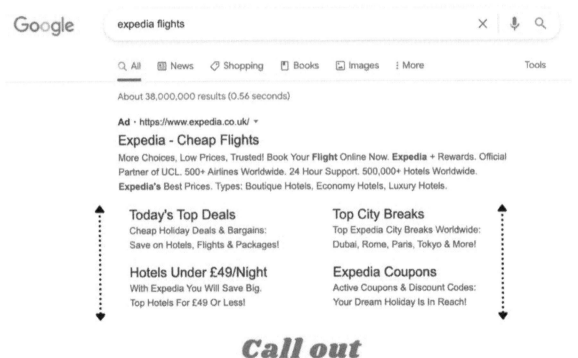

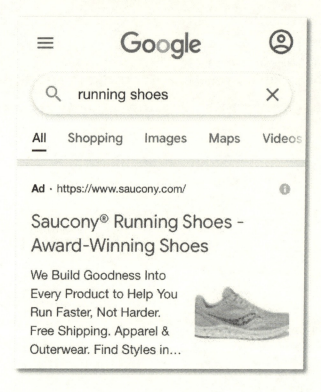

This will then lead you to the next step of creating ad groups. Ad groups are like containers which will have your keywords and ads. Ideally:

- Max of 7-10 ad groups per campaign
- Max of 50 keywords per ad group
- 2-3 ads per ad group including one responsive ad

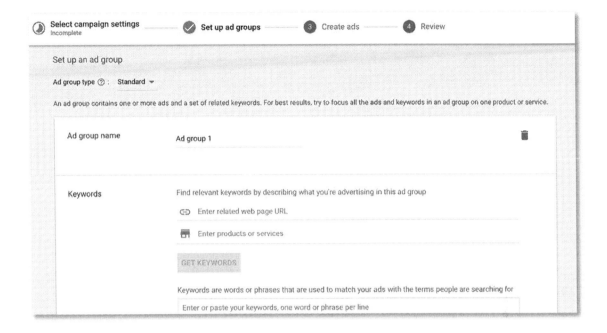

Now this is the fun part where you will incorporate all of your selected keywords. On this you have noticed that there is matching type mentioned which is key to define how broad or exact you want to bid on a user's query.

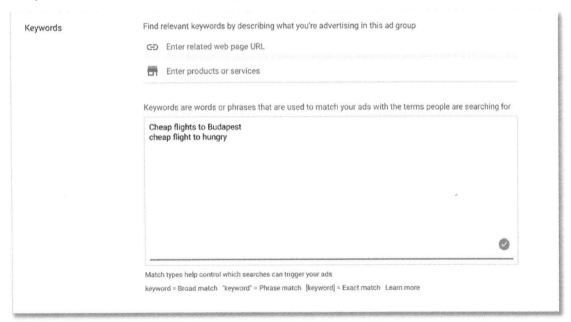

The next and final part is ad creation where you will have the opportunity to show offers, services, your unique selling points and more about your business. There is a character limit in each section so give some thought as to what you want to say on the headline and what you want to highlight on the description.

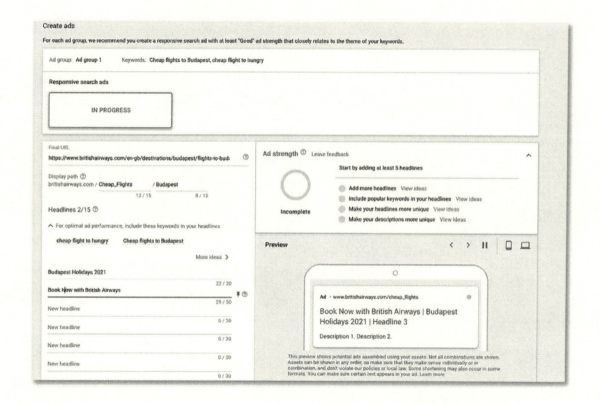

## Ads on Google Search has the following components:

### *Standard Ad*

- Headline 1- 30 characters
- Headline 2- 30 characters
- Headline 3- 30 characters
- Display Path- (Display URL)- 15 characters
- Description 1- 90 characters
- Description 2- 90 characters

## Include keywords in Ad text for best results

It is always a best practice to include core keywords within ad copy. Keywords which mirror a user's search query will perform well. Any relevance of keywords which you are bidding for and are in the ad copy achieve good click through rates. For example, if you have the keywords "cheap holidays to Paris," your headlines you can include "cheap holidays" in ad copies.

The final part of campaign building will be to review and publish where you will get the chance to look at everything carefully before your campaign goes live. Google normally takes 24 hours before you start seeing any clicks or impressions.

## Check if your ads are live on Google

It is important to check if your search ads are live or not. There could be many reasons your ad is not live, so it is always a good idea to check. One of the prime methods is to go on your

**Google Ads > Tools > Planning > Ad diagnosis**

You can insert keywords, set the location and device, and then see if your ad is live. Google will highlight your ads in green. Sometimes, if you run out of budget during the day, you might not see your ad, and for that, double check your daily budget.

**In a nutshell, this should be your account structure.**

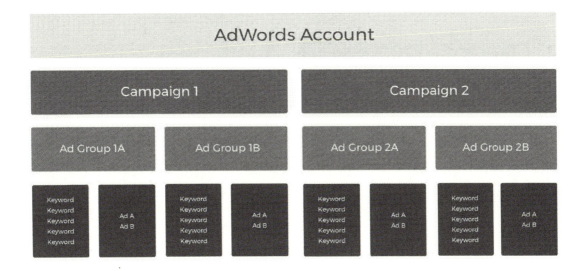

# 11

# GOOGLE DISPLAY NETWORK

# GOOGLE DISPLAY NETWORK

**In Chapter 11 you will learn:**

- *What is Google Display Network - GDN*
- *How GDN works*
- *Benefits of advertising on GDN*
- *Display creative options*
- *Re-marketing concept*
- *How to build your first GDN campaign*
- *Google Tag manager*

In simple words, the Google Display Network is a collection of millions of websites under the Google Ad Sense Program where you as an advertiser can place ads (web banners or text ads on various websites) through Google Ads. Any web banner you see while visiting the CNN website or Movie Reviews site is part of the display network.

Since users spend a lot of time reading content on different websites every day, content creators or publishers get the chance to make money by selling those ad spaces to brands through the Google Display Network. Obviously, Google charges to bring advertisers to publishers as a cut as well as charges advertisers to place ads to make money as the middle man. While a Google search is to reach intent-based audiences, with Google Display Network, you can reach millions of websites.

Google is a technology-based company so innovation is part of its DNA, hence it is making progress every year. Over a period of time, advertisers can now place ads on websites based on demographics, geo location, and based on devices, which was not possible initially when this platform was introduced.

With sophisticated targeting options backed with Google Machine Learning, you can now target users based on interests.

**Affinity Audience**
With a choice of more than 80 groups based on interests, such as hobbies or interests in auto, you can now reach different pre-defined audiences.

**In-market segments**
Users actively looking for shopping can be reached, for example: people buying shoes but are interested in a particular shoe type.

## How Google Display Network Works

In a simple way, there are 3 parties involved.

Publisher or website owner who owns and runs the site can be a part of the Google Ad Sense Program.

Advertiser or brand pays Google to bring traffic to site. They have to set up campaign via Google Ads.

Google via Google Ad Sense Program which allows the reach out to potential buyers.

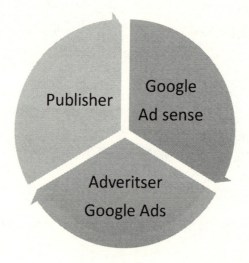

## Who is making Money $$$?

Publisher sells the space based on agreed CPM rates and will be paid by Google.

Advertiser pays Google for clicks or impressions to bring traffic to site.

Google make money by getting commission from publisher.

## Be aware that Google has monopoly

It is a well-known fact that Google has monopoly in almost all countries except China and Russia, so how do we know that Google has a conflict of interest? In reality, it has a conflict of interest as it is gaining in monetary terms in every aspect whether sending traffic to a website or charging advertisers. In every case, Google has the winning situation.

This is a discussion within the industry and Google has its own explanations. In my more than 11 years of digital marketing experience, every advertising medium has its own pros and cons. For example, outdoor advertising is very expensive and targeted to everyone or at mass level, whereas TV gives some kind of targeting options. Similarly, with Google campaigns, you need to make judgement based on rational and not spend money if campaigns are not working. We spend hundreds of thousands of dollars each year with great return on investments across Google platforms.

# Why still advertise on Google Display Network – GDN?

**Brand Awareness**

By combining the three major platforms, i.e., Search, Display and YouTube, you can build brand awareness. Even small companies are now in a position to advertise with a limited budget which was not possible 20 years back. With brand awareness, you can run continuous ads for constant messaging and brand recall across the user journey.

**Niche targeting**

Advertisers can now reach almost any type of audience. You can target people who are interested in classic music or adventures to the North Pole. This is a great way to do targeted ads with customised messaging.

**Reach users when they are browsing**

Reaching at mass level to potential users or buyers is possible on GDN. Users' browsing content across different sites can be reached with flexibility like the time of the day or even at device level.

# The positive & negative sides of Google Display Network - GDN

On the positive side, it is a great platform to access millions of potential users while they are browsing content to show your products or services. The flip side is that if you don't understand how the whole system works, you can easily lose your money and you will be devastated. I have helped many brands to grow their reach, traffic and even conversions through Google Display Network, but this needs a few steps to be taken first.

First things first, know your audience, meaning you need to know exactly to whom you want to reach out to. For example, a bank wanting to promote mortgage services to first time buyers can make a *customer persona*.

- Age – 25 to 35 years old
- Gender - male and female (single or joint applicants)
- Income - salary from £30k or above
- Working class – both white and blue colour jobs
- Geo - living in London – in flats or shared accommodation
- Young couples recently starting a new life

All this information now helps you to start your audience research on Google Display Network. One way to approach this audience is to find websites or blogs where people talk about how to get first time mortgages; information and experiences shared by others is like a social proof so selecting those sites will help you to place bank products in front of first time buyers. You can select an audience in two ways, either select the number of websites and place ads, or through keywords, let Google Network find the relevant websites and place ads. First method is safer as you know exactly where you will be showing your ads, what kind of website it is, what type of banner placement they offer and the quality of traffic.

## The online customer journey is not straightforward

Remember, a customer's journey is not simple or linear; people do take time to think, research, ask friends, read blogs and compare the quality of a price before they hit the final check out button. During this whole buying process, Google Display Network can provide a chance to introduce your brand through creative web banners with pictures, graphics and call to action. This is what we call an upper funnel audience, so if your company has a budget, do try it.

# Display creative options on GDN

Google Display Network provides various options to show your graphics ads, for example, these are some creative options available:

- Responsive Display Ads - *Highly recommended*
- Banners - HTML-5 - JPG or GIF as picture (e.g. 300x250 unit or 728x90 unit)
- Out stream ads
- Native ads
- In banner ads - video
- Skippable or non-skippable ads as video (if site has video content)

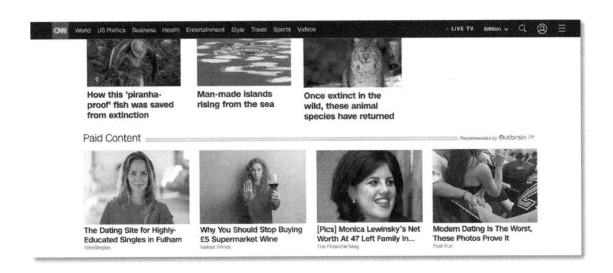

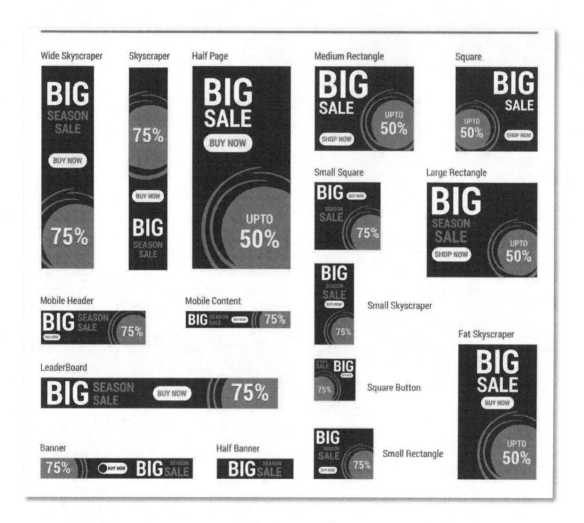

## Remarketing – *Give it one more chance*

Remarketing is a way to connect with potential customers who have previously interacted with your website. It allows you to strategically position your ads in front of these audiences as they browse Google or its partner websites across Google Display Network, thus helping you increase your chances to offer discounts or remind those audiences to make a purchase.

## Benefits of Remarketing

Whether you're looking to drive online sales, increase sign ups or promote the awareness of your brand, remarketing can be a strategic part of your campaigns. These are a few benefits of using remarketing:

### Well-timed targeting

People who have previously visited your site and browsed through different products can be shown your ads and offerings while they are searching elsewhere. This way you can remind them and maybe offer personalised offerings like a 10% discount as they are more likely to purchase. This is a great way to pursue your potential customers.

**Targeted Advertising**

Customer segmentation is a proven method to reach out to people based on various factors like age, demographic or recent browsing behaviour. Google remarketing allows you to create various remarketing lists, which I am going to tell you in a simple process in the next section. With the creation of remarketing lists, you can remarket people who have visited certain sections of your website or even the ones who added products to their basket but did not check out.

**Reach At Scale**

Through remarketing, you can easily scale your efforts across various websites, apps or video networks. You can reach people on your remarketing lists across their devices as they browse over 2 million websites and mobile apps. Ideally, you will need at least 1000 cookies before you can start remarketing campaigns.

**Ad Creation is Easy**

Google Ads can easily create ads via a free ad gallery, all you need is a few high quality, engaging pictures, texts or content about your offerings and any USP you can promote. The process is easy and made for anyone who has little knowledge of using computers.

# Setup your first Display Campaign - GDN

**Targeting by keywords**

The first thing to be aware of is that the default settings to create a display campaign is both search and display network. I would advise not to use both—just stick to GDN only.

Log in to your Google Ads account and click on the plus sign under campaigns.

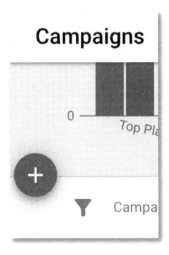

Click on the + plus sign for new campaign.

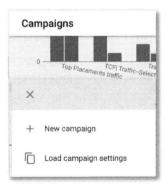

Select your campaigns objective as this is the important part of your strategy. If you select brand awareness as an objective, then Google Ads will show your banners to increase your brand awareness and brand recall. You can't expect traffic on-site with this objective so think about what you want to achieve from your campaign.

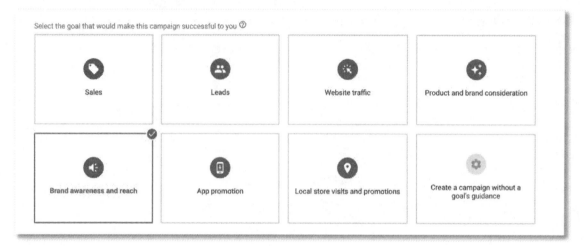

The next step is to select Network. At this stage, only select Display Network. This will allow you to show on ads-only websites.

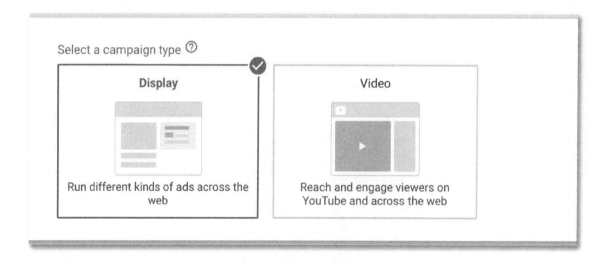

Name your campaign so that you can remember what type of ads or campaign objectives you are running. Once you have multiple campaigns, this will help you identify them based on objective or type. For example, brand awareness - product name.

Location settings allows you to select country, city, post or zip code or even at a radius level. This is an important part as sometimes tight regional targeting will not serve ads, and if you choose too broad an area, you might spend part of your budget on areas where you are not providing services or you don't have a potential customer base.

...es you want to reach out to specific communities who speak more than one ... For example, English and Spanish (Hispanic), so you can select both or just select English.

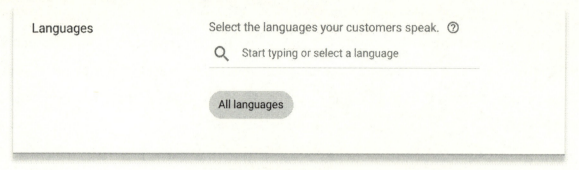

As the whole Google Ads model is based on bidding between advertisers, this part is important.

**If you want users to take a direct action on your site like sign up or purchase** and you're using conversion tracking, it may be best to focus on conversions.

**If your objective is to generate traffic to your website**, focusing on clicks could be ideal for you. Cost-per-click (CPC) bidding may be right for your campaign.

**If you want to increase brand awareness** focusing on impressions only, you can use cost-per-thousand viewable impressions (vCPM) bidding to put your message in front of customers.

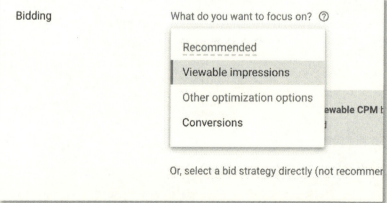

The next stage is to set your daily budget. Google will distribute this budget across the entire day. Sometimes your budget will be spent before the 24 hours is up; that means there is more impressions or ad inventory available, but your budget is limited. This also means that you can reach more users online by increasing your daily budget. Your average daily budget can sometimes also be underspent and sometimes overspent by 20% or more, so keep an eye on daily basis.

```
Budget          Enter the average you want to spend each day
                £ 30
```

Depending upon business hours or online behaviour, you can schedule ads for certain times of the day or even certain days of the week. For example, if you know that your potential customers are more likely to convert in the evening, you can schedule ads from 5 pm onwards until midnight. Here you can also select the start and end date of the campaign.

```
Ad schedule     All days        ▼  00:00     to  00:00
                ADD

                Based on account time zone: (GMT-04:00) Eastern Time
                Saving this removes the settings you changed and adds new one:
                performance data

Start and end dates    Start date
                       Jun 10, 2021      ▼

                       End date
                       ● None
                       ○ Select a date   ▼
```

Google also gives you the flexibility to choose how you want to run ads. For now, just select optimise best performing ads.

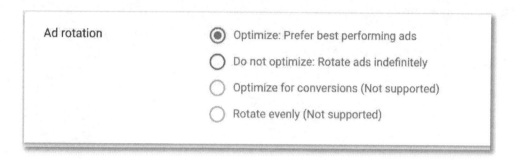

This is a very important part from a brand safety point of view. Here you can exclude sites and content type where you don't want your ads shown. Exclude everything which you think is best for your company or for your client's brand. The internet is full of junk and weird websites so make sure you've excluded those at account level.

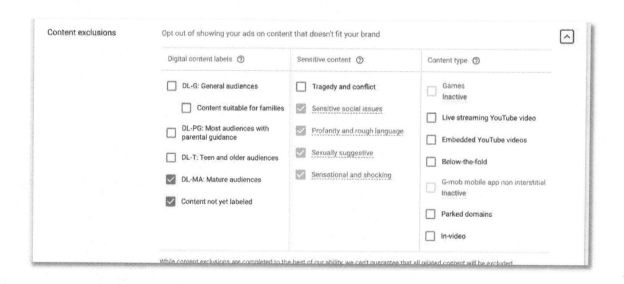

As most of people use mobile devices on the go and consume content on a day-to-day basis, here you can select which devices you want to target, even operating systems like Android or even mobile models like the iPhone 10. This granular targeting will allow you to reach certain types of audiences.

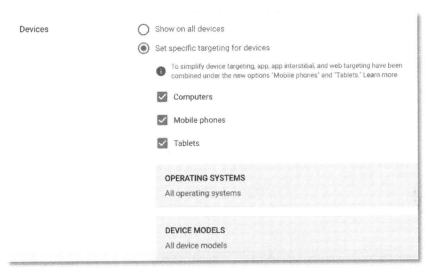

Leave this step for now if you are making this campaign for the first time.

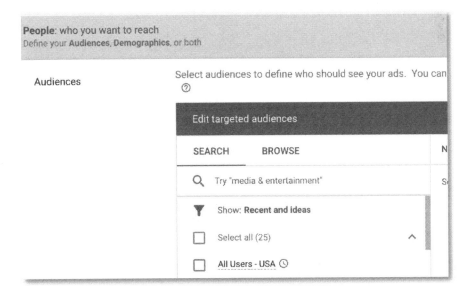

For now, we will add keywords to target users on Google Display Network. I will explain the other two methods, i.e., topics and placements, separately. If you have search campaigns running for various products, you can then download that in an excel sheet, and Google will try to match those keywords with the website content.

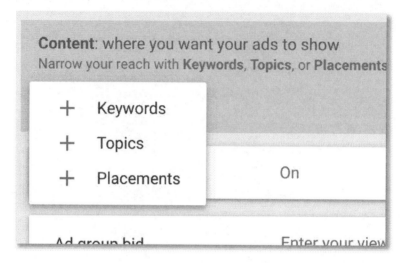

Once you enter keywords, you will be able to see how many impressions are available. Here you can go slightly broader as unlike search network, Google display network is not as precise.

In this step, you need to set the 'Ad group bid' to how much you are willing to pay for 1000 impressions. So, start the CPM bid at £1 and see if ads are serving. Increase the bid by 20% in case you see no impressions. Bidding really depends on the industry and the level of competition, so for example, we know the travel industry is competitive, so you might start from £3 to see the actual CPM and then start adjusting or reducing based on the results.

| Ad group bid | Enter your viewable CPM bid for this ad group ⓘ |
|---|---|
|  | £ 3 |

Ad creation is the last step in the campaign creation, and here Google will give you a few options to upload ready-made banners or copy existing ones. I would recommend having at least one responsive ad with your own products pictures and ad text.

**Create your ads**
Create an ad now, or skip this step and create one later. Your campaign won't run without an ad.

- ＋ Responsive display ad
- ⬆ Upload display ads
- ▭ Copy existing ads

This is the last and final step.

There are a few other targeting methods available on GDN to reach out to potential customers. In our above example, we have shown you how to setup keyword-based campaigns, but there two more methods worth mentioning. As a beginner, you don't need to go beyond these targeting methods.

## Targeting by Audiences & Remarketing – *Best Opportunity for Advertisers*

Through pre-defined audiences within Google Ads, you can now target users who have already visited your site. You must have noticed when you've visited a John Lewis site and didn't buy anything or left during the purchase process that a display banner would start chasing you anywhere you went on the internet. This is called remarketing. Remarketing provides a second chance to show relevant offers to someone who knows your brand, who has already been to your site and who has gone through the initial process of research, so it is good idea to chase them and reinforce your message to encourage them to buy.

**The Buying Cycle Is Not The Same For Every Product**

Remarketing also comes in handy and useful when an online customer journey is complex or when buying high value goods such as cars, houses or even expensive long-haul flights or cruises. Taking for example holidays from the UK to Orlando, USA, to visit all the Disney parks is a big financial commitment for a family, so they will definitely do detailed research and take their time before committing to booking a holiday. We are talking about a commitment of £15,000 for a 15-day holidays (family of 4) to see all parks and universal studios.

*Note: Remarketing to certain categories is not available, such as faith-based content, guns sales or drugs/pharma products.*

## How to create remarketing lists

A remarketing list is a collection of website visitors or app users gathered by snippets of code (tags) added to your site or app. Every time users visit your site, Google tag them through web browsers like Google Chrome and paste cookies on their device. This way, you start collecting lots of cookies which are actually just anonymous users' data who have recently interacted with your site. By law, Google can't collect personal information, so it is kind of safe.

In order to build remarketing campaigns, you need to have a remarketing list so that you can use the same to target audiences. There are few simple steps to create a remarketing list, and I would advise that as soon as you start your first campaign, install Google tags as well as make a remarketing list. This list can be made through the audience manager under Google Ads (one of the tabs). All you need to specify is which website page you want to track, what the time period is for or membership duration and a few other things. Once the list is created and starting to populate cookies, you can then add your list to your remarketing campaigns.

In summary, you have to tag your site either via audiences or enable remarketing within Google Analytics via Tag Manager and cross link with Google Ads to Google Tag Manager.

# Use Google tag manager to verify - *Google Tag Assistant*

Once your tag is installed, use the free Chrome extension tool to verify whether your tag or code is working or not. It will take a few days before you can see the numbers, but it really depends on the website regular traffic. You can check as to how your list or number of lists are doing by going to Google Ads > Tools > Audiences.

Google extension will allow you to quickly see if your codes are working or if it has some issues.

**Google Tag Assistant**

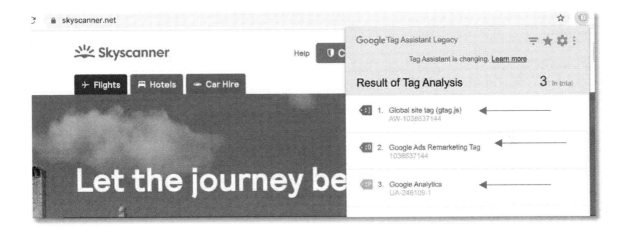

## Remarketing list size

- Google Display Network - at least 100 active visitors or users within the last 30 days.
- Google Search Network - at least 1,000 active visitors or users within the last 30 days.
- YouTube must have a minimum of 1,000 active visitors or users within the last 30 days.
- Gmail ads must have a minimum of 1,000 active visitors or users within the last 30 days in the Display Network.
- Discovery ads must have a minimum of 1,000 active visitors or users within the last 30 days.

## Membership duration

Membership durations can be set for 30 days as a default, but I recommend having the maximum days of 540 so that you can keep using cookies whenever needed.

| Network | Default duration | Max. duration |
| --- | --- | --- |
| Display Network | 30 days | 540 days |
| Google search | 30 days | 540 days |

*Note: You can set any limit from 7 days to up to 540 days. For example, you can create cookie list for checkout shoppers for the last 7 days or 15 days. This 30 days is default option set by Google.*

## Remarketing Strategy for beginners

Step 1: Make display campaign with either consideration or conversions as an objective.

Step 2: To begin with, start your campaign with different ad groups for each list. For example, visitors on home page, people who visited products pages and visitors who did not check out.

Step 3: Have at least 5 main HTML- 5 banners for desktops and 3 for mobile devices.

Step 4: Create one display responsive ad.

Step 5: Set frequency capping for one user to 3 per ad group each day. This will ensure that the ad will not show again and again to the same user, and you will not overspend.

Step 6: Exclude all categories which you don't want to opt into to show ads such as adult content.

Step 7: Review your campaign after 48 hours against impressions, CTR, CPC and conversions, if any. Remarketing campaigns take a little time to take off and depend on the list of your cookie size.

## remarketing campaigns

By now you have understood the concept of remarketing, why it is used, how to create a remarketing list and some basic strategies, so let's build your first remarketing campaign.

The process remains the same where you will select your campaign's objective, select display network, target location, bid, and budget, but when it comes to adding an audience, this is where you can add your audience list. Remember, targeting on display network sets at ad group level where you can have different types of audiences within different ad groups.

For example, one ad group contain a remarketing list with the ad group name of all visitors and other ad groups who left the shopping cart on the last stage. This way you have the control to set bids, budgets and separate creative banners for different types of audience lists. In reality, not all customers are the same; some are more important than others, and remarketing can be a good solution.

**Go to Tools > Audience**, and here you can see the remarketing list. In our example, we will add all users from the USA who have visited our site.

| Audience name | Type | Members status | Size: Search | Size: YouTube | Size: Display | Size: Gmail campaign |
|---|---|---|---|---|---|---|
| *In use* | | | | | | |
| AdWords optimized list — Combined audience based on available data sources | Combined list Automatically created | Open | <1,000 Too small to serve | <1,000 Too small to serve | <1,000 | <1,000 Too small to serve |
| All Users - USA — All Users | Website visitors | Open | 1,900 | 1,900 | 1,400 | 410 Too small to serve |
| | | | 67 | 67 | 56 | 7 |

So, at the campaign's creation process when selecting audience, you will see this list.

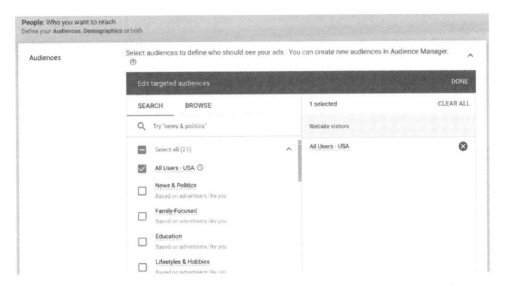

**Lookalike or Similar Audiences to Expand your reach**

Once Google Machine Learnings has enough data, i.e., remarketing lists, it can then start looking for users with similar online behaviour. This is a great way to expand your reach with a similar audience, but as a beginner, I would strongly recommend not trying this strategy. This is good for when you have certain level of experience and ample budget to play with.

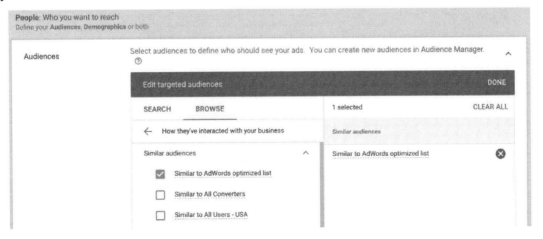

## Double check and verify your targeting method

Once you have a number of search, display and video campaigns running, it is sometimes difficult to keep track as to which campaign has what type of audience and objectives. It is always a good habit to double check your campaign settings.

## Basic Optimization for remarketing – *Bids, Frequency Cap, Budget & Site exclusions*

From an optimization point of view, it is a good idea to set a frequency cap as you don't want to show the same ad to the same users more than 2 or 3 times a day. Set ad group bids and budgets based on priority, for example, people who have left the final page of cart are more important, so they need to bid on higher compared to anyone who has landed on your home page. Always exclude site exclusion and category exclusion as you don't want to show your ads on certain sites (adult or rough language).

### Targeting by Placements (websites)

This is the simplest method as you will already have some idea of websites where you want to show ads. Either make a list of those site ad uploads or you can search within the campaign creation process. Under content targeting, you can choose placements. Insert keywords and then click on the website. Here you can see holiday sites where you can place ads with the potential impressions available per week.

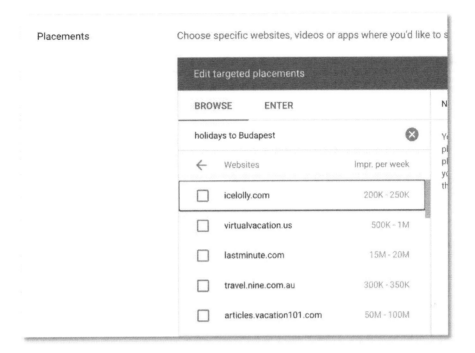

**Gmail Campaigns**

Google owns Gmail and it is one of the most popular email tools used by billions of people around the globe. Since this service at a basic level is free if you don't buy storage space, its popularity has grown in the last 10 years. This will give an extra edge to Google to include Gmail as a part of Google Display Network. This means you can now show ads to Gmail users while they are reading their emails. Imagine you are arranging a family reunion after many years and discussing various possibilities of booking a theme park at some kind of resort. While exchanging emails with your siblings, you start noticing Centre Parcs offers. This kind of targeting can be possible within Gmail campaigns.

The process is the same, i.e., select your objective, or no objective, and then select the campaign type. Here you can see option as Discovery Ads (run your ads within Gmail and YouTube).

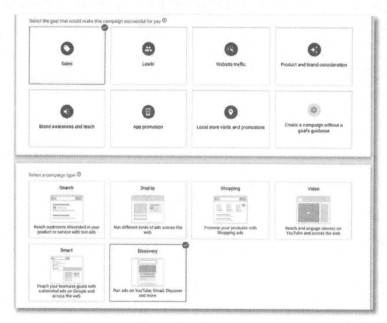

For Gmail campaigns, you need to upload various pictures and text as the format is slightly different from website banners. Targeting can be done based on the following methods:

**Keywords targeting**

You can select certain keywords related to your industry and target those. For example, holidays or vacations can be targeted as your ads will be shown to users who are actively talking about holidays.

**Audience targeting**

You can remarket to users who have already been to your site and chase them when they are using Gmail.

# 12

# YOUTUBE VIDEO NETWORK

# YOUTUBE VIDEO NETWORK

**In Chapter 12 you will learn:**

- *What is YouTube advertising?*
- *True view formats*
- *Buying models*
- *Ad creative choices*
- *How to build your first YouTube campaign*

YouTube is the second-largest search engine after Google and the number one video content site. Bought in 2006, it is a Google subsidiary, which means that it is owned and operated by Google. Every month, more than 1 billion people visit YouTube and watch over 6 billion hours of YouTube videos. These are huge numbers and will allow you to reach your customers on YouTube by topics, keywords or demographics, like "women under 35" etc. This give brands a huge opportunity to showcase their products through engaging video ads. So just like Search and Display ads, you can also place videos and banners across YouTube.

## Why use YouTube Ads?

There are many benefits of using video marketing and here are few to quickly go through. There are 3 main reasons for you to advertise on YouTube:

1. People are watching video content every day
2. They are searching for topics – "how to" or "help videos"
3. If you already have a cookie pool, you can re-engage with them through video ads

**Video advertising is a popular tool to reach mass audiences**

In recent years, especially with the popularity of Smart TVs and cheap mobile data packages, smart phone penetration and video consumption has increased. Video advertising is now part of every media plan, and brands want to tell their stories, promote their products and engage with customers on this platform.

## Top of Mind Approach - *Find your customers, followers & supporters*

Whether you have a music channel, review videos or celebrity endorsements, YouTube works for everyone. From How To videos to *Khan Academy*, YouTube has changed the lives of many people, both in terms of giving a platform to earn money but also to learn.
Every day, people watch videos of thousands of topics, and through YouTube ads, you can easily target them.

Suppose you are promoting holidays for Europe by targeting residents of San Francisco area. There are plenty of travel video channels whereby you can show your ads. All you need to do is start typing a few words and phrases on YouTube and you will see the top videos and channels. Scrutinise each based on popularity and start making a list. Once you have handful of sites, you can then make a placement campaign on YouTube by targeting, age, gender, location and devices. This is just a simple example as I will go through the step-by-step process of how to build different types of YouTube campaigns. If you already have Google display ads running, you can remarket to your same audience with video ads.

## How to find relevant content for your brand

Relevancy is everything when it comes to digital marketing, and YouTube is no different. Like Google Keywords Planner, YouTube does not have any tools, but there are ways to find out relevant content, videos or sites.

YouTube auto-complete - this is the great way to start. Start writing something and you will see a lot of suggestions. See screenshot for *Holidays to Europe.*
You can use Reach Planner if that is allowed for your account.

*Use Reach Planner – if this option is visible in Google Ads tools*

One of the ways to find popular videos is by finding out the popularity and see which videos have the highest volume. Another way is to go by genre, for example, you can browse videos based on categories like fashion, sports or music. There is no set rule as you know your brand better, and see which videos or channels are more appropriate. Popular on YouTube can give you a quick view of the currently trending videos, for example, if you are selling fidget spinners and that's something appearing on the trending page, it is good an idea to promote your product here.

It is very easy to get trapped on YouTube by spending hours to find videos, but at the same time, don't target any channel which is very generic. For example, people do like music, but everyone's taste is different, so you need to make sure that you have some kind of targeting layer or niche.

The first few seconds matters – *So make good YouTube Ads*

Unfortunately, our attention span is very limited when it comes to using social media. People decide within the first 5 seconds whether they want to continue watching the video or skip it. This is a very challenging aspect from a marketing point of view as imagine you've made your product video and launched your YouTube campaign, but it has a low view rate of 10%. You have done your research for the audience, set the right bidding and made the right video title, but it is not working. So, making an engaging and catchy video ad is the most important aspect of video advertising.

- The first few seconds must be catchy.
- The video needs to tell a story that connects user.
- And most importantly, should have call to action.
- Make sure you use all clickable links on your video, give enough information on the description with URL and have the right video tags so that it helps the YouTube search engine to find your video.

## Create Cards in Your Videos - *Call to action*

YouTube's cards are a free tool and great way to drive traffic to your site. Tesco has used cards to promote Food Factory, while Chef was using same machine in one of the cooking recipes. So, as soon as Chef started using Food Factory, the card popped out on the right side with an image of the product and clickable to website to buy with the offer.

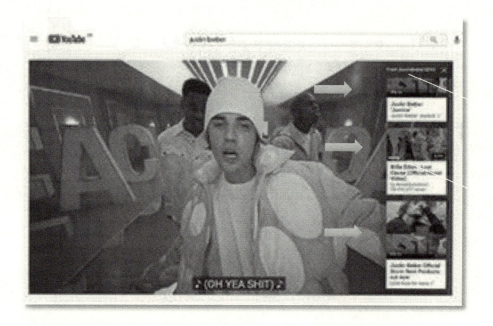

Before we jump to making YouTube campaigns, it is important to know what type of ad formats we can use and in which situation.

# True view formats - *Ad formats for YouTube*

Depending on your goal, you can use different ad formats built for YouTube. These ad formats are:

## Skippable in-stream ads

This is the most common type of ad format. Video ads can appear before, during or after videos across the YouTube network. If a user skips an ad within the first 5 sec, this is where you need to make sure your ad is catchy.

**Non-skippable in-stream ads**

These are non-skippable ads, and generally YouTube charges a bit more for these types of ads. It is for 15 second or less ads.

**Bumper ads**

6 second bumper ads are also a non-skippable format, and it is a good format for brand recall.

**Video discovery ads**

Recently, video discovery ads have got popularity as ads appear when users are searching proactively on YouTube through keywords. These are similar to Google Ads where you pay on a CPC basis and are more action led.

**Buying models on YouTube**

Skippable true view ads are sold on a cost per view basis, whereas non-skippable formats like 6 second bumpers and 15 second are on a CPM basis.

# How to build your first YouTube campaign

## *Step by step guide*

In order to build a YouTube campaign, you need to make sure that you have uploaded your video or video ad onto your official YouTube channel. Without that, Google Ads will not allow you to build a video campaign, so this is the prerequisite.

Secondly, it is also a good idea to link your Google Ads account with your YouTube channel so that you can get metrics as well as collect cookies to market later on. It means that anyone who watched or viewed your video on your channel can be chased later through remarketing campaigns.

Click on the plus sign to create a campaign. On the next screen, select your campaign's objective. For now, we will build a brand awareness focused campaign. The next step is to select the network, which is YouTube.

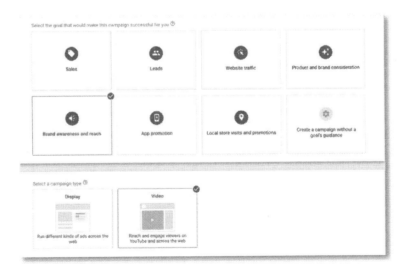

The next step is to select the campaign sub type. Here you have an opportunity to select what kind of YouTube ad format or ad type you want to run. There are different options like bumper ads or non-skippable and selecting each ad format should have an objective. For example, a 6 second bumper is good for top of mind or brand recall, and skippable in-stream is good for initial brand awareness.

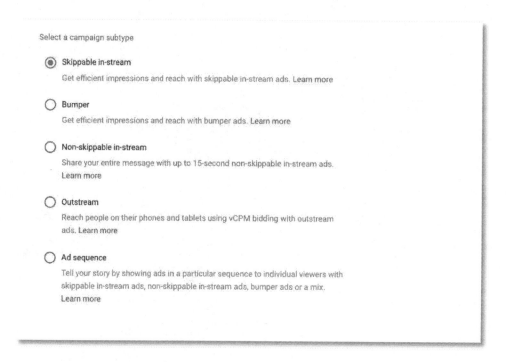

Within the general settings, name your campaign and allocate either a daily or total campaign budget with a start and end date.

By default, both video partners on display network is selected by Google Ads, so make sure you un-check this option and only select YouTube videos for now. The default settings are not ideal as the majority of your spend will be on display network instead of YouTube.

Make sure at this stage you only select standard inventory as this will have a major impact on your budget spend as well as brand safety. With expanded inventory, there is a risk of your ads showing on sites which has graphic violence or nudity, whereas with limited inventory, your reach might be limited.

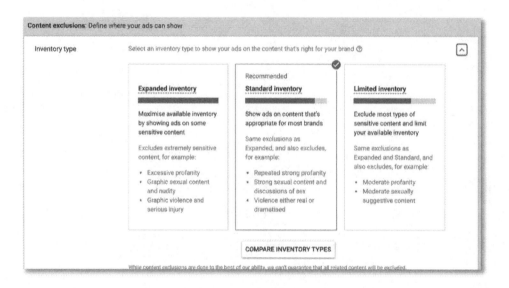

Here you can also exclude being shown on certain type of contents, for example, content with parental guidelines or live streaming videos.

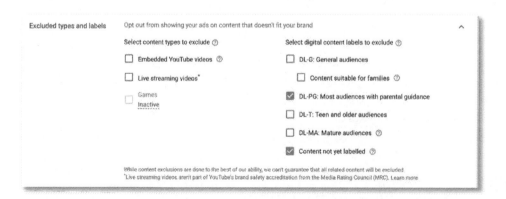

The next step is to select the account level conversion and devices. You might only want to show your ads on desktops and on Smart TVs, so select devices based on your target audience and goals.

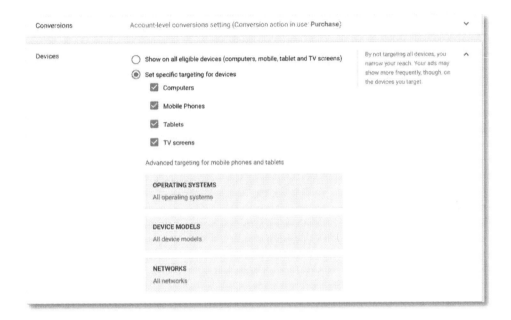

If you have a limited budget, make sure you set some level of control in terms of how many times you want to show the same ads to the same users and how many times a day. There is no set rule, but you can start to view cap 3 per day and see if your ads are serving or not. If you notice that ads are not serving and budget is not being spent, then increase this to view cap daily to 5 per day.

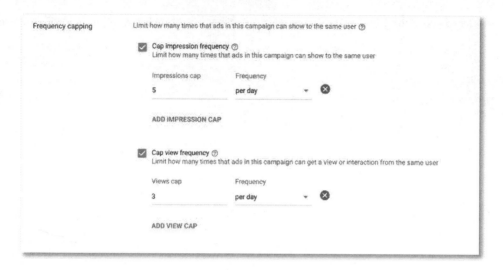

Here you can select the age and gender based on your products. For example, European holidays from USA might not be suitable for an 18-24 age group, so choose what is the best option for your product or services.

Audiences are groups of people with specific interests, intents and demographics as estimated by Google, so you can select predefined categories, for example, people who are interested in travel.

There are other methods for targeting which I am not going to explain now. These are:

1. Targeting by keywords – same as GDN
2. Targeting by placements- same as GDN
3. Targeting by topics
4. Remarketing – same as GDN

The next step is to set your CPM bid (amount you are willing to pay) and your video ad (URL from YouTube channel).

This is the final step where you can review and publish your video campaign.

# Facing problems - Get Google's Help !

You can ask for help from Google teams from different sources and in different situations. For example, your ads might get rejected or you need to discuss billing.

## Help Section within Google Ads

Once you log into Google Ads, you will see the help section under the question mark icon in the top right-hand side of the screen. Click on it and you can see the ways to find help in your country.

## Live Chat and email Help

A live chat section is also available under the same section.

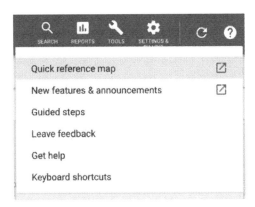

# 13

# GOOGLE ANALYTICS & METRICS

# GOOGLE ANALYTICS

**In Chapter 13 you will learn:**

- *The importance of Google analytics*
- *Key metrics in Google analytics*
- *Top Google Analytics reports*

Think: Google Ads is one side of the coin; the other side is Google Analytics. Without looking at data and doing the right analysis in Google Analytics, your campaigns will not produce the desired results. So, what exactly is Google Analytics? In simple terms, it is a web analytics service that track and reports on website traffic. Google analytics was launched in 2005, and since then, it has become one of the most commonly used analytics services. Its basic version is free, so anyone can use it by installing small codes from the website.

In order to use Google Analytics, you need to create an account first and then generate a code which you can place on your website or client website. It is also a good idea to link your Google Ads with your Google Analytics account so that the cost data and campaigns data can start reflecting within analytics. Remember: more accurate data will lead to better decisions.

## Important metrics in Google analytics

Tracking data and then analysing it is one of the important tasks for digital marketers. Google Analytics can track hundreds of metrics, such as how many users visited the site, how much time they spent (bounce rate) and whether they have completed the goals (sales). These are some popular metrics:
- **Users** - A person who interacts with an app or site.
- **Bounce rate** – The bounce rate is single-page sessions divided by all sessions.
- **Sessions** - The period of time a user is active on your site or app.
- **Goal** - A setting that allows you to track the valuable actions or conversions that happen on your site or mobile app.
- **Page views** - A page view is an instance of a page being loaded (or reloaded) in a browser.

**Metrics vs. dimensions**

Every report in Google Analytics is made up of dimensions and metrics.

Dimensions are attributes of data. For example, the dimension CITY specifies the city, for example, "London" or "Paris," from which a session originates. The dimension PAGE indicates the URL of a page that is viewed.

Metrics are quantitative measurements. The metric SESSIONS is the total number of sessions. Google Analytics reports consist of dimensions and metrics. Understanding the difference between them is critical for proper understanding of reports.

Dimensions can be customized in Google Analytics. Examples of common dimensions include: Language, browser type, city and country, models of devices and user age group.

# The 10 most useful Google Analytics reports

These are the top reports you should have a good idea of before you begin your Google Analytics journey.

**Audience Overview**

An audience report provides a high level summary in one place. It shows aggregated data like the number of users, how many pages they visited, the average session and bounce rate.

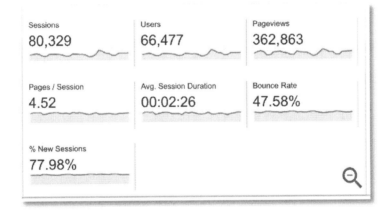

## Demographics

Demographic data provides information about the age and gender of users. This report shows which age group is performing better overall along with other metrics like the conversion rate, number of transactions and the average order value.

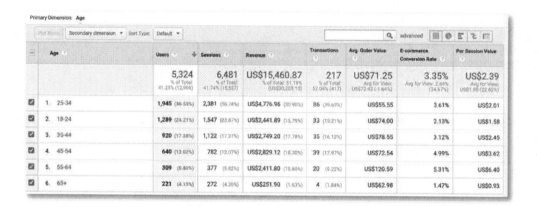

## Site Content

The site content reports are very useful for finding out how your content is performing.

All Pages: engagement metrics for each page on your site.

Content Drilldown: engagement metrics for directories and pages on your site.

Landing Pages: Acquisition, behaviour and conversion metrics for the landing pages on your site. See whether your landing pages are engaging enough for users and contributing to conversions the way you want.

Exit pages: exit metrics for the last pages users open on your site. See if users are exiting your site from the pages you expect (e.g., a checkout page).

## New vs Returning Users

As per Google Analytics, anyone who visits your website for the first time and have never been to your website as per Google Snippet is a new user. Since it is a cookie-based metric, sometimes if a user is coming back from different device, they will be treated as first time visitor.

Returning visitors is someone who visited again will be recorded as per Google Snippet. There is no set ratio but 65% new and 35% return is a normal split.

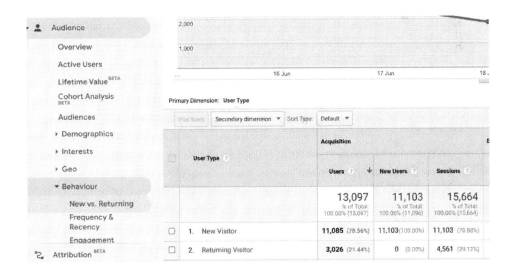

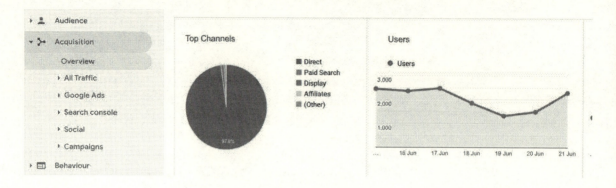

**Channels**

Users on your website can visit from any source. As a customer journey is not straight forward, Google Analytics has pre-defined channels.

1. Direct - When a user types the URL into the browser
2. Organic Search - When a user clicks on search engine result pages (not paid ad)
3. Social - When a user visits from Facebook, Instagram or YouTube
4. Email - Traffic generated from email broadcast.
5. Affiliates - Any affiliates sending traffic to your site
6. Referrals - Any other display site sending traffic
7. Paid Search - Traffic from paid ads like search, display or YouTube
8. Other Advertising

## Source/Medium

Source is the origin of the website from where a user visited your site. If people come from a Facebook page, it will be classified as social or Facebook as a source.

Medium is a category of traffic defined in Google Analytics. For example, traffic coming from paid campaigns, i.e., CPC or PPC.

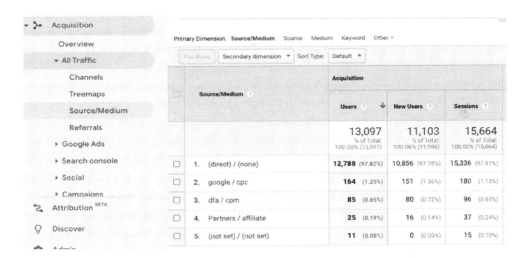

## Landing Pages

It is the first page users view in any session. It shows which pages are popular for users to enter into your site.

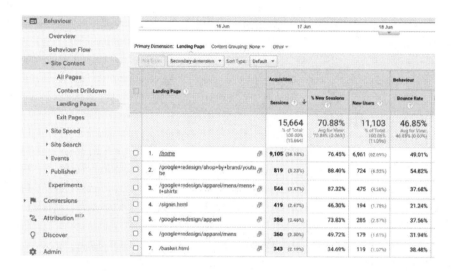

## Acquisition Overview

This report gives you an overview of the overall performance of various traffic sources, channels and their behaviour towards set goals, such as conversions (sales).

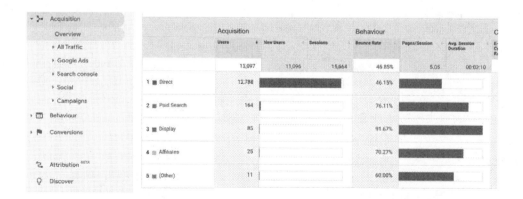

## Top Conversion Paths

Top conversion paths is great way of finding your most popular referral paths and how many times users interacted with each marketing channel before converting on your site.

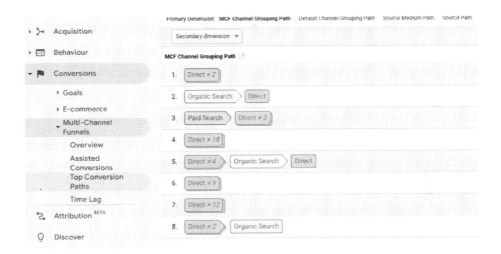

## Assisted Conversions

One conversion can take many steps and involves many channels. Assisted conversion is a Google measure other than the last click.

# Google Ads Key Metrics To understand

### CPC - Cost-per-click

A very common term used on a day-to-day basis; PPC or pay per click advertising. Cost-per-click (CPC) bidding means that you pay for each click on your ad when someone clicks on it. For PPC or CPC bidding campaigns, you set a maximum cost-per-click bid – or simply "max. CPC" – that's the highest amount that you're willing to pay for a click on your ad, and in reality, it is based on competition.

### CTR - Click through rate

Perhaps the most basic metric to see as soon as you launch your PPC campaigns. Simply, it shows how many times your ad is shown and how many users ends up clicking on it. It is shown in ratio, so for example, if your ad is shown 100 times and only 5 users click, your CTR would be 5%.

*Formula*

Clicks ÷ Impressions = CTR.

For example, if you had 5 clicks and 100 impressions, your CTR would be 5%.

### CPM - cost per mile or cost per thousand impressions

This is a buying model and way to pay to show your banner ads 1000 times on a website or app. It is a traditional way of paying for your ads or banners inventories. Similar to TV ads where we buy on CPT, CPM is the most common metric used in media buying.

## CPV - Cost per view

A bidding method for video campaigns where you pay for a view. A view is counted when a viewer watches your video ad or interacts with the ad, whichever comes first. Video interactions include clicks on the call-to-action overlays (CTAs), cards or companion banners. You set CPV bids to tell Google the maximum amount you're willing to pay for each view.

## Impressions

Each time your ads appear on Google searches or Google Display Network, an impression is counted. It is a very useful metric to know about your ad performance, as if your ads do not appear, how could you expect clicks to site.

## Impression share

It is the percentage of impressions your ads receive compared to the total number of impressions.

**Impression share = impressions/total eligible impressions**

Impression share is a good metric to understand whether your ads might reach more people if you increased your bid or budget.

## Interactions

This is the main user action which is associated with ad format, for example, clicks to sites or views for video ads, or calls from users on call extensions.

## Daily Budget

At campaign level when you set a daily budget, that means it is the average amount you set to spend per day. Google will optimise your campaign spend for days or months when you are most likely to get clicks or conversions. Remember, on some days, budget spend might be 20% more than what is set for each day, and this is normal.

## Conversion

Conversion means customer or user takes action as per your set goals. It could be sales, leads, sign up, event registration or visits on offer page. This is one of the most important metrics to look at on a regular basis as better conversion a rate means more sales.

## Cost per conversion or cost per acquisition – CPA

A CPA metric is one of the most important KPIs for any digital campaigns. It is an average amount you have paid to acquire one sale. It is calculated by dividing the total cost by the number of sales or conversions. For example, if your ad receives two conversions, one costing £2.00 and one costing £6.00, your average CPA for those conversions is £4.00.

## Conversion Rate

It is calculated by taking the number of conversions and dividing the number with total ad interactions. For example, if you had 25 conversions from 1,000 interactions, your conversion rate would be 2.5%, since 25 ÷ 1,000 = 2.5%. A better conversion rate means more visitors converting into sales.

## ROAS - Return on ad spend

This bidding strategy lets advertisers bid based on target return on ad spend. To use the ROAS bidding model, you need at least 15 conversions, ideally within the past 30 days or prior.

# 14

# CAMPAIGN OPTIMISATION PRACTICAL TIPS & TRICKS

# CAMPAIGN OPTIMISATION

**In Chapter 14 you will learn:**

- *Google Ads (campaigns) optimisation*
- *Key tactics and insights*

1. If your campaign is not serving any impressions, it means you are not competitive enough to be appear in the ad auction. So, increase your bid by 20% and see in the next 24 to 48 hours.
2. Have separate campaigns for each product you offer to have more control on the budget and to gauge performance.
3. Always separate ad groups based on themes and keyword matching strategies, for example, phrase, broad or exact match.
4. Try not to have more than 50 keywords in one ad group.
5. Try to improve the quality score of each keyword with better CTR and landing page experience. Group high performing keywords in one ad group, for example, above QS 5 in one ad group.
6. Responsive search ads with a good score perform well.
7. Use all extensions to get more real estate on page one.
8. Ad site links are great, but change them from time to time with new offers on description. Try to get at least 4 ad sitelinks on brand ads.

9. Give regular looks at ad auction reports to see your performance in comparison with competitors.
10. Use automate functions/rules but be careful and put a thought process in before having any automated rules. For example, you can increase the budget by 20% for campaigns when it is achieving more than a 5% conversion rate.
11. Do optimise campaigns based on age and gender. Not all audiences perform the same for every product so keep looking at best performing age group.
12. Location targeting - Try to opt in for targeting in Google Display Network, i.e., presence; people in or regularly in your targeted locations.
13. Always have frequency capping as there is no point in showing the same ads to the same user multiple times in a day. This will waste your budget.
14. Bidding: Start from enhanced CPC and then move on to other bidding strategies once you have more than 20 conversions.
15. Content exclusions: Make sure your brand is safe and always show ads on the right sites, so apply content exclusions, for example, don't show ads on sexually suggestive sites.
16. Always have remarketing lists to collect data. Set membership durations to the max, i.e., 540 days.
17. Ad rotation: Start with the best performing ads and then see what is working for you.
18. Always have display response ads as this will allow your ads to appear across GDN with various ad formats available.
19. Devices: Device targeting works well if you have mobile optimised site. Keep looking for which devices are performing well for conversions and then adjust bids.
20. Unless needed, exclude apps targeting across GDN. This will save your budget.
21. Link Google Analytics with Google Ads, and Google Ads with YouTube to collect data.
22. Be careful of using a similar audience; try with a small pool first.

23. Use Google Trends to find out trending patterns for keywords, products or services.
24. Always install Google conversion tracking codes on websites. This will allow you to see eCommerce conversion rates and sales.
25. Wait 48 hours at least when making any major changes like a bid or new ad.
26. Some display campaigns will take one to two weeks for a learning period, so give that time before making decisions. Google Machine Learnings need data to collect and analyse before it starts performing.
27. Try Smart Campaign to see if that works for you but with a reasonable budget and time.
28. Always look at the correct metrics to gauge campaign performance, for example: if a campaign is set to get impressions, then traffic or clicks is not something you should look as a base metric.
29. Once you've got more than 20 conversions, try a maximum conversion bidding strategy. This strategy works well if you have decent budget to scale. We have seen great results with a maximum conversion bidding strategy.
30. YouTube 6 second bumper ads can be bought on a CPM basis.
31. YouTube skippable ads can be bought on a cost per view basis.
32. If you have campaigns for more than 2 months, try CPA campaigns. This will allow you to control your cost per acquisition vs sales and profit margin. Start CPA with Google recommended then reduce gradually where possible.

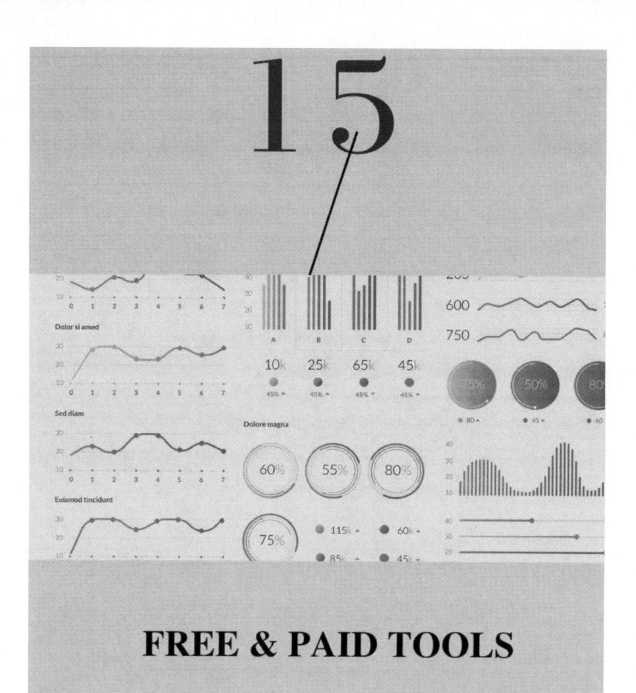

# 15

# FREE & PAID TOOLS

# FREE & PAID TOOLS

## In Chapter 15 you will learn:

*Top free and paid analytics and tools*

The internet is full of free and paid resources about Google Ads, like blogs, videos and various websites. I have listed a few resources which I've used over the years. Most of them are free so feel free to use and experience them yourself.

**Google Official Ads Help Centre**
https://support.Google.com/Google-ads/
This is an easy-to-use resource portal from Google. For the beginner to advanced users, you will find lot of information.

**Learn with Google - Videos**
https://www.youtube.com/user/learnwithGoogle
Google YouTube channel has a number of videos on different topics to learn and practise.

**Google Partners Help Centre**
If you work as an agency, it is the best source to get an official Google badge and client's incentives.
https://www.Google.com/partners/become-a-partner/

## Google Grants for Non-Profits

https://www.Google.co.uk/intl/en/grants/

If you are a registered charity or non-profit, you can apply for the Google Grants program to get free funds of $10,000 every month.

## Skill shop by Google

**https://skillshop.withGoogle.com/**

It's an official Google training portal for if you want to learn and get certifications in search, display, video and analytics.

## YouTube Advertising

**https://www.youtube.com/ads/**

A wealth of information about YouTube advertising for anyone who wants to learn video ads.

## Ubersuggest Keywork tool

**https://neilpatel.com/ubersuggest/**

Keywords research tool, but it's paid, so make sure before getting a subscription if you need it or if you can try a free trial first.

## Google Ads Editor

https://ads.Google.com/home/tools/ads-editor/

It's a free tool which can be download, and you can work offline and publish later on. Agencies and large client's tasks can be done with bulk changes which is increasing efficiency.

## SEM Rush

https://www.semrush.com/

A paid tool equally good for SEO and paid ad campaigns. SEM Rush can be used for keywords research and for competitor's analysis.

## Occam's Razor - Google Analytics

https://www.kaushik.net/avinash/

If you want to brush up your Google Analytics skills, this blog from Avinash is a great help. He has explained everything in a very simple way.

## Google Trends

https://trends.Google.com/trends

A useful tool to find out current and past trends for searches across Google.

## Search Engine Land

https://searchengineland.com/library/Google/Google-ads

A digital marketing blog with news and expert opinions from industry leaders. The latest developments in Google Ads can be found here from time to time, so it's good to visit this site often.

# GLOSSARY

**CPM**

Cost Per 1,000 Impressions. You are charged per 1,000 times your ad is shown, based on your bid.

**CPV**

Cost-per-view (CPV) bidding is the default way to set the amount that you'll pay for your TrueView video ads

**CPC**

Cost Per Click. You are charged each time a user clicks on your ad, based on your bid.

**CPA**

The average amount that you've been charged for a conversion from your ad. Average cost per action (CPA) is calculated by dividing the total cost of conversions by the total number of conversions.

**OVP**

A positioning statement that explains what benefit you provide and how you do it uniquely well

**CTR**

CTR is the number of clicks that your ad receives divided by the number of times your ad is shown: clicks ÷ impressions

## Cookies

A small file saved on people's computers to help store preferences and other information that's used on webpages that they visit.

## Tags

Tags are segments of code provided by analytics, marketing, and support vendors to help you integrate their products into your websites or mobile apps

## GDN

A group of more than 2 million websites, videos, and apps where your ads can appear.

## URL

The location of a webpage or file on the Internet. Some of Google's URLs include *www.google.com*

## CTA

A call to action (CTA) is a prompt on a website that tells the user to take some specified action. .

# ABOUT THE AUTHOR

**Hassan Imtiazi - MA, FIDM, MCIM**

Hassan is a Digital Marketing veteran who has helped grow many brands over the last 16 years. After spending nearly a decade working in digital for multimillion dollar brands in the UK, USA & ME, Hassan knows what truly drives conversions and activates brands online. Hassan has helped many clients to grow and generate more than $70 million in revenue.

Google has published two case studies on his work. Hassan holds an MA in International Business from the University of Northumbria in Newcastle, UK. Hassan also has a Completed Certificate & Postgrad diploma in Digital from IDM-UK and Certificate in Brand Building from Judge Business School at Cambridge University.

Hassan Imtiazi

# THE END

Made in the USA
Columbia, SC
04 October 2023